MW01181268

Black Women, Feminism and Black Liberation:
Which way?

Vivian V. Gordon

p.29-lynching

36?

Third World Press

Third printing 1991

ISBN 0-88378-108-9 (paper)

Manufactured in the United States of America

Third World Press
7524 South Cottage Grove Ave.
Chicago, IL 60619

Cover design by Cheryl Catlin

They need something to believe in
the young
That is only part of the truth
They need a map and a guide
to the interior

If we have the Word let us
say it
If we have the Word let us
BE it
If we have the Word let us
DO

They need something to believe in

Mari Evans
NIGHTSTAR, 1981

Dedication

This book is dedicated to my mother, Susie R. Verdell and to the women of my extended family who have provided my support network over the years.

Felicia Anderson,* Cleopatra Armstrong, Ruth Baker,* Evelyn Berry, Anne Boone, Marietta Cephas, Edna Colson, Elizabeth Cooper, Wyonella Cotman, Margaret Dabney, Margarite Davies,* Myrtle Dunn, Georgia Gordon,* Lucille Green, Grace Harris, Johnnella Jackson,* Lillian Jenkins, Hermione King, Hortense Macklin, Emily Madden, Nannie McDaniel, Amaza Meredeth,* Virginia Miller, Undine Moore, Goldie Nicholas, Eunice Robbins,* Elizabeth Saunders, Dannie Townes,* Margaret Worthington and Mary McCloud Bethune.* (*deceased)

ACKNOWLEDGEMENTS

Research assistance, critical comments and encouragement were generously given by Lois Smith Owens. In particular, Lois has called to my attention some of the issues crucial to African American Women who are single parents raising male children. Lois's reflective thoughts about personal struggle and her frank exchange have been vital to me in the formation of many of the ideas presented here.

The first edition of this book emerged during an especially difficult time for me at the University of Virginia. The critical comments, support and encouragement of persons of my network there will never be forgotten. In particular, I wish to acknowledge and to thank: Jamal Koram, Hortense Hinton, Karen Chandler, Hope Wilson, Art Brooks and William Harris.

In this second edition of a book about African American women and the liberation struggle, it is important to again acknowledge several liberated men who continue to have an impact upon my thinking. Several of these men are relatively new friends; others are friends over a 25-year span of time. I continue to be encouraged to conduct research and to report through clear, open, and candid discussion by: Haki R. Madhubuti, poet, activist and editor, Third World Press; Molefi K. Asante, dynamic theorist, scholar and author; Ja Jahannes who has a quick and creative mind as he works to teach and encourage research about the Black experience; and, Reuben R. McDaniel, Sr., my dear friend and "brother" since childhood. These men may well laugh as they read and think about my transformations which my current publications reflect. I caution them to laugh softly, for I have seen tremendous transformations in them as they have been about the business of liberation which

i

includes freedom from sexism. The emergence of these liberated men is in no small manner directly related to the quality of the women to whom they are married, and the women with whom they work and interact.

Many dynamic Black women in higher education have influenced my thinking through their research, through informal conversations (over terrible, overpriced meals) at conferences, and through their lives. There is an increasing commitment to research that directly touches on the lives of Black women by such women in higher education.

I do not know the names of the many Black sisters with whom I have talked at the bus stop, in the market, or at the ice cream counter in the shopping center where we seek relief from the heated temperatures of the weather and our daily lives. As a person often prejudged to be a "bourgeoise Black professor," I know them and who came to know me as a sister in the struggle, although we often fight in different arenas.

My perspectives have undoubtedly been influenced by my students from whom I continue to learn; especially those who have stayed *long* hours after class, or have trailed down the halls with me in heated debate. I thank them for calling me at my home to say "quick, turn on the TV" and for bringing to class books, tapes, and clippings (as well as visiting family and friends) that speak to issues over which we have differed. Since the initiation of this book and the second printing, my past students at the State University of New York at Albany and Wellesley College as the sources of joy for teaching in Black Studies. This is of particular importance as regrettably, far too many students continue to avoid and to negate the value of courses specifically concerned about the Black experience as taught from an Afrocentric theoretical and methodological orientation.

Like the first edition, this very brief work is overburdened with acknowledgments; however, my more recent experiences in higher education have been especially traumatic. If I have sustained and if I continue to bring information and to promote a desire to learn, it is clearly because of the student encouragement and support I have received.

I continue to move forward having been sustained by many "of the kinship." My treasures increase.

I assume full responsibility for the information presented here. I hope that I have clearly and accurately presented the work by others to whom I make reference. I hope that errors are few.

Vivian V. Gordon
February, 1987

CONTENTS

Figures:

Tables:

PREFACE

Many Black women have questioned the viability of a Black/White women's coalition in the social movement called women's liberation. To ask "could it work," or "does it make sense," or "can we trust," among other questions is not new. Often, however, such questions must be posed in muted tones, for to openly question a Black/White woman's coalition is to incur sanction as a Black woman afraid that some White woman will "get her man." Others presume that those who question such a coalition are ignorant or naive about an economically structured social inequality. Such attitudes have not only come from some Black men, but also from some Black women who are already devoted supporters of the national women's movement. The Black woman who questions Black/White coalitions is presumed not to have thought seriously about the matter, or to be responding only on the basis of anti-White woman emotions. Hopefully, this work will underscore the serious thinking and the socio-historic research as well as some creative didactic relationships which have immediacy for decisions about Black/White women's coalitions.

The need for open and frank exchange about the range of factors that critically limit progress by Black women and African American communities increase as additional years come and go -- each leaving in its wake a continued number of psychologically, as well as socio-economically, devastated Black Americans. For example, within the African American community there are increased numbers of single parent families, the majority of which are headed by women. Limited attention has been given to the multitude of factors which contribute to this situation, including Black male sexual politics as an indicator of frustrations and power moves by those denied the means to accomplish the greater society's role requirements of male as dominant provider and protector. It is much easier to focus only on the number of women-without-men-families and to mislabel the African American community a matriarchal society.

Clearly, the issue of single parent families is one of the most crucial issues before the Black community. However, without frank self-group discussions about specific factors, band-aid solutions based on stereotypes will prevail. When we look at the factors which impact upon the lives of many Black children -- especially those of single parent families headed by women -- we must clearly identify the primary enemies of such children to be: racism, sexism and economic oppression. These are the factors that contribute to Black community limitations and to the Black woman as a triple victim. One must question how mothers could be expected to perform adequately the nurturing/teaching role when, in their provider role, they are in constant battle against multiphase oppression.

As we develop new strategies for change, there is a need to recognize and admire the resilience of those women who, while under three-fold attack, have continued to provide early childhood care centered in an environment of nurturance and love. To address women's issues, therefore, is not only to address the crucial needs of Black women, it is also to address the historic primacy of the African and African American community; that is, the primacy of its children and their preparation for the responsibilities and privileges of mature personhood. From this perspective, it becomes even more apparent that only enlightened emancipated women and men can be co-workers against those limiting factors that are imposed upon the African diaspora in America and throughout the world.

This work proposes to contribute to an analysis of the viability of Black/White women's coalitions. A coalition schematic is presented to illustrate the pervasive powerlessness of African American and other non-White women. The power relationships illustrated by the schema can be translated from Black women in America to the sisters of a troubled Africa still emerging from cultural devastation and forced change away from male/female partnerships centered in extended family communities. The schema illustrates the situation as might be applied to Black sisters of Latin American communities who also must confront cultural destruction and poverty centered in racism and sexism; and the sisters who face similar situations throughout Europe as well as the most acute conditions of such women in the Middle East.

Women of the African diaspora are the primary transmitters of the culture. If that culture is truly of value; if we would perpetuate that which has been good in the relationships between Black men and women; if we would take individual action against the new forms of non-White destruction, then we must be willing to confront issues through both critical analysis, and a reflective review of the socio-historic record. This is the pattern of the discussion that follows.

In particular, those of us in academia must contribute to the development of theoretical perspectives which allow for a movement away from a locked-in application of models and paradigms developed for an Eurocentric society to Afrocentric beliefs and lifestyles. This work is an attempt to make a small contribution to that effort. If it upsets some, blatantly irritates others and prompts loud "Amens" from many, it will have accomplished some of its purpose. Its primary purpose, however, is to help establish a position which can provide a point of departure for the determination of African American participation in, and support for, efforts to bring about change through the process of organized social movements. Appropriately, the work concludes with some suggestions about what some persons can do *now*.

A part of this work was presented to the 1983 Chicago, Illinois Conference on the Black Woman sponsored by the Caucus of Black Women, Northeastern Illinois University Center for Inner City Studies. I would welcome critiques and responses.

BLACK WOMEN, FEMINISM AND BLACK LIBERATION: WHICH WAY?

Overview

The purpose of this work is to review briefly the difference in the nature of the oppression of African American women and Euro-American women who again call to Black women for full participation in the movement popularly known as women's liberation. The position presented here that a Black woman's coalition with a White woman dominated movement centered around an Eurocentric focus holds the potential for an isolation of Black women from the promised rewards of the coalition as well as an isolation from their historic identity and efforts in behalf of the liberation of the African American community.

In support of this contention, we shall consider: (1) traditional coalition theory, (2) the emergence of women's studies programs, (3) the Black woman as a victim of a trilogy of oppression, (4) the socio-historic record of Black/White female relationships, (5) status and color conflict among Black women, (6) feminism and imposed definitions for Black female/male relationships, (7) economic inequality by race and sex, (8) Black women's organized efforts against racism and sexism, (9) the present and future struggle: A typology of attitudes, (10) directions for change in Black female/male relationships, and (11) some conclusion.

The position presented here will no doubt be loudly condemned by some who point to a so-called common oppression of all women and thereby proclaim that this oppression is the basis for a Black/White women's coalition. This group considers gender to be the salient issue. Others will view this work to present an anti-White posture that will only contribute to a greater conflict between Black and White women. However, that is because such people do not understand that the motivation for this work reaches beyond the potential for further cleavage in an already highly polarized racist society to other concerns which permits a clear focus upon the issue of the viability of a Black/White women's coalition as a means for socio-political and economic gains for Black women and the Black community.

Many Black Americans are increasingly distressed by the obvious surrender of much within the Black community to a promise of a "better situation" through integration -- which, for the dominant group, usually means movement from a Black culture into White conformity, -- and which has often failed in its rewards to Black people even where reported to have taken place. Moreover, it would appear that the integrative process provides little hope for real changes in the immediate future, but encourages the additional losses of vital African American talent and resources.

Social change must begin with self definition, especially among the youth who must establish firm roots if they are to sustain in the battle that seeks to render them powerless. From this perspective, it becomes apparent that Black women and the Black community must carefully scrutinize appeals from White dominated movements with Eurocentric underpinnings. Black women who identify with the women's liberation movement will internalize the rhetoric and perspective of that movement and become alienated from themselves (self-hate), and alienated from the race, as well as from a splendid record of activities against racism. It is important, therefore, that any focus on African American women be evaluated to determine the collective benefits or losses to the African American community, even when the short-range goals might hold obvious benefits for Black women.

Traditional Coalition Perspectives and Black/White Women's Issues

Traditional coalition theory underscores the necessity for a strategic evaluation of the basic power in the *reward phase* of the effort as a requirement for partnership, if there would be a meaningful and nondestructive achievement for the component with the *lesser power*. When one considers the relative posture of Black and White women, and the accompanying dynamics of their linkages, one clearly must view the direct White female/male power linkages as they have historically existed and as they continue to exist today. Such linkages result from ethnicity, marriage and a shared "othergroup" philosophy. As the coalition schema illustrates (see page 5), a Black/White female coalition represents an ill-fitted choice for African American women.

The more obvious coalition dynamic would be between the various non-White American "third world" women. That such a coalition is fraught with difficulties is a further indication of the extent to which minority women have, all too often, internalized the white-good/black-bad self-associations which represent the religiopolitical ideologies of the dominant group.[1] The inability of American non-White women to establish long-term and meaningful coalitions is a complex topic to be addressed by a different paper.[2]

The schema assumes the following situation to exist in the nation: (1) dominant economic and socio-political power concentrated within White America (the collective White ethnic) with the White male holding the monopoly; (2) a sharing in that White male power by his primary group, i.e., the family and its relationships; (3) power by White women either independently or by virtue of their linkages to White men; (4) international economic and socio-political power linkages between White American males and females resulting from historic conditions of war conquests, colonialization, economic investments, and various contemporary manifestations of a philosophy of manifest destiny.

The limited linkages, where such exist, between African Americans in general, and Black women in particular, are dramatized by broken lines in the schema. These relatively weak socio-economic and political linkages between non-White people in general, African and American Black women, may be viewed to be supported by the following: (1) the absence of any continuous, clearly defined linkages between the African American and non-White international communities; (2) within the nation, an ongoing denial of African origins and the accompanying kinship between African Americans and Africans; (3) limited contemporary and historic support for pan-Africanism; (4) limited focus on the African diaspora in studies about the African American experience; (5) limited dialogue and association between Africans in America and African Americans, especially among students and faculty in higher education; and (6) the manipulated or orchestrated conflict between African American and other non-White minorities who continue to compete with each other for limited economic and socio-political resources.

5

Figure 1.

The Gordon Schema

Power Relations and Potential Coalitions: A View of African American, Other Non-White and Euro-American Women

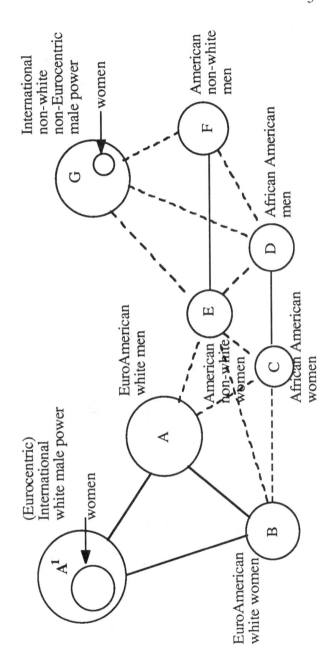

6

Figures 2 - 6
Non-White/White Power Relationships
Selected Categories

Figure 2.

A.   <u>Economic Domination</u>

	A^1	A	B	C	D	E	F	G		
A^1	-	0	1	1	1	1	1	1	|	6
A	1	-	1	1	1	1	1	1	|	7
B	0	0	-	1	1	1	1	0	|	4
C	**0**	**0**	**0**	**-**	**0**	**0**	**0**	**0**	|	**0**
D	0	0	0	1	-	1	0	0	|	2
E	**0**	**0**	**0**	**0**	**0**	**-**	**0**	**0**	|	**0**
F	0	0	0	1	1	1	-	0	|	3
G	?	0	1	1	1	1	1	-	|	5

C and E represent the most economically dominated, and thus, powerless groups.

Key:

A^1 - International Eurocentric White Male Power
A - Euro-American White Men
B - Euro-American White Women
C - African American Women
D - African American Men
E - Other Non-White American Women
F - Other Non-White American Men
G - International Non-White/Non-Eurocentric Male Power

Figure 3.

B. Political Dominance

	A¹	A	B	C	D	E	F	G		
A¹	-	0	1	1	1	1	1	0	|	5
A	0	-	1	1	1	1	1	0	|	5
B	0	0	-	1	1	1	1	0	|	4
C	**0**	**0**	**0**	**-**	**0**	**0**	**0**	**0**	|	**0**
D	0	0	$^1/_2$	1	1	-	0	0	|	$2^1/_2$
E	**0**	**0**	**0**	**0**	**0**	**-**	**0**	**0**	|	**0**
F	0	0	$^1/_2$	$^1/_2$	0	$^1/_2$	$^1/_2$	-	|	2
G	0	0	$^1/_2$	$^1/_2$	0	$^1/_2$	$^1/_2$	-	|	2

C and D represent the most politically dominated groups. D's limited political strength reflects the greater total number of Black male elected officials compared to C and E.

Figure 4.

C. Cultural Domination

Control over education, the media, and primary institutional values

	A¹	A	B	C	D	E	F	G		
A¹	-	0	0	1	1	1	1	0	|	4
A	1	-		1	1	1	1	0	|	6
B	-	-	-	1	1	1	1	0	|	4
C	**0**	**0**	**0**	**-**	**0**	**0**	**0**	**0**	|	**0**
D	0	0	0	-	-	0	0	0	|	0
E	**0**	**0**	**0**	**0**	**0**	**-**	**-**	**0**	|	**0**
F	0	0	0	0	0	-	-	0	|	0
G	0	0	0	0	0	0	0	-	|	0

A maintains the highest level of cultural domination through control over education, the media and primary institutional values. B shares the culture of A¹ and A. None of the non-white groups are in a dominant culture position. They do not control the media and their own educational programs.

Figure 5.

D. Physical Domination

The potential for body abuse.

	A^1	A	B	C	D	E	F	G		
A^1	-	0	1	1	$^1/_2$	1	$^1/_2$		|	4
A	0	-	1	1	$^1/_2$	1	$^1/_2$		|	4
B	0	0	-	$^1/_2$	$^1/_2$	$^1/_2$	$^1/_2$		|	4
C	0	0	0	-	0	0	0		|	0
D	0	0	$^1/_4$	1	-	$^1/_2$	0		|	$1^3/_4$
E	0	0	0	0	0	-	0		|	0
F	0	0	$^1/_4$	1	0	1	-		|	$2^1/_4$
G	not salient								|	

The fear of reprisal by A^1 and A limits the potential for D and F to exercise power over B. D and F are not able to provide equal protection for C and E from A^1 or A or B as B may impart upon A or A^1 against C and E, or as B may be guilty through complicity, as was the case during slavery.

Key:

A^1 - International Eurocentric White Male Power

A - Euro-American White Men

B - Euro-American White Women

C - African American Women

D - African American Men

E - Other Non-White American Women

F - Other Non-White American Men

G - International Non-White/Non-Eurocentric Male Power

Figure 6.

E. Military Power

Control by para-military or military forces within the nation.

	A¹	A	B	C	D	E	F	G	
A¹	-	0	1	1	1	1	1		5
A	0	-	1	1	1	1	1		5
B	0	0	-	$\frac{1}{2}$	$\frac{1}{2}$	$\frac{1}{2}$	$\frac{1}{2}$		2
C	0	0	0	-	0	0	0		0
D	0	0	0	0	-	0	0		0
E	0	0	0	0	0	-	0		0
F	0	0	0	0	0	0	-		0
G	not salient								

In this situation G is again not salient. In the sense that B shares in or benefits from the control A¹ and A are able to exercise, B has the potential for strength in this arena. Although C D E and F are represented in the military structure they have limited control.

Note: The most frequent comment about the coalition schematic and the power diagrams is that the representation for G (Figure 1) should be much smaller in proportion to A¹ and that the non-White women's power within G should be about one-half the strength represented. Even if these changes were to be made, the basic contention would be sustained. In fact, the basic thought would be enhanced.

Given this situation, traditional coalition theory would presume linkages between C and B, advocated by C who has less power than both B and A. However, what traditional coalition theory does not consider is that although B reports domination by A and a desire to loosen the AB linkage, in fact, B is bound to A as a result of shared economic and socio-political benefits through marriage, social and intimate relationships as well as a shared belief system; in particular, a shared belief about C. B's linkages with A result from the role complex of wife, mother, sister, daughter and primary sex partner. It could be argued that in these traditional sex-linked roles, B as primary socializer of the children perpetuates the belief system of A and B about C.

There is no viable coalition between B and C, or A and C. Traditional theory might underscore that for C some small gains resulting from a CB coalition would be better than no gains. However, this perspective does not consider the nature of C's caste by virtue of color. Nor does such a perspective give attention to the *nature* of the power dimension in Black/White relationships in America. Power concedes to power and only to the extent necessary to maintain power. Moreover, power extracts a heavy toll for small concessions. For example, to achieve limited economic and socio-political gains from B, and especially from A, C is required to surrender important linkages of identity, self-group value, and traditions, as well as positive social and intimate relationships with African American men, D. C would be required to become a further victim of anglo-conformity (cultural imperialism). Such conformity would ultimately result in the destruction of the African American community and culture, especially since for that culture C is the primary transmitter and socializer.

In decisions about the ultimate outcome of a BC or AC coalition (though AC would be unlikely), C must maintain an awareness of the extent to which, in America, race remains a caste/class stigma which limits upward mobility for non-Whites. There is limited equal interaction even for those persons presumed to have accomplished upward mobility through socio-economic achievements.

"...if minorities are not in mutual contact, have very diverse cultures and economic interests, and have a previous history of intense competition of conflict with one another, then one may expect that the degree of mutual trust and communication among them will be too low to overcome the normal resistances to cooperation... Closely related to previous minority contact and competition is the question of how the minorities are ranked along some relatively distinct hierarchy of prestige of power. This, too, is likely to be linked to whatever are the predominant lines of social cleavage within the society... Degree of similarity to the dominant group is also likely to be a strong correlate of position in the hierarchy. If C is more similar to A and B than is D, C will have a vested interest in emphasizing its differences with D and its similarity to A. A, in turn, is likely to differentiate itself from all three minorities unless, of course, it finds it necessary from time to time form a conservative coalition with B against C and D, or with B and C against D.

... Most important, perhaps, is the extent to which the minorities perceive themselves to be in a 'zero-sum' competition in which the gains of one group must always be made at the expense of another. On the other hand, minorities may perceive themselves as being in a 'positive-sum' situation in which the gains of one add to the gains of all, making a coalition more desirable."[3]

The contemporary literature which addresses social movements tends to move away from the traditional coalition thinking represented by the Gordon schematic and places a focus upon the mobilization of resources to bring about change. From this perspective, we could consider it reasonable for African American women to form *time-limited, issue-specific* coalitions with White women. It is *only* within these parameters that a Black/White women's coalition, such as that required by Jesse Jackson through his "rainbow coalition" could be accomplished. Emphasis is given to the time-limited, issue-specific nature of such a White-Non-White women's coalition, for many Black women of today remember the extent to which a similar "rainbow-type" coalition in the 1960's resulted in the displacement of Black women by White women from key positions in the movement. Jackson stated that he would consider the selection of a woman vice presidential runningmate. Hopefully, he would have selected a third world American woman. Black male leadership must recognize the extent to which they often extend to White women in political coalitions and show themselves to be insensitive to Black women -- the very women from whose wombs and nurturing they emerged.

As is established later by this paper, White women have historically and consistently *welcomed Black men* into organizational efforts while at the same time *excluding Black women*. Had his support been more extensive, Jackson would have been in a unique position to reverse past trends and to make a statement to all people about the recognized abilities, activities and political acumen of African American women, and other women of color so often neglected by the political world.

After a look at the life conditions of Black women and those of the general Black community; exchange with dynamic and concerned Black women from a range of socio-economic backgrounds; and exchange with Black women scholars contributing to research and the historic evaluation of the Black womans' experience, one can only conclude that there are some dynamic incompatibilities between African American women and feminism as advocated by the women's liberation movement.

African American women are one of the most victimized and understatus groups in the nation. It is important that the gains which have been so painfully accomplished not be put into jeopardy through a scattering of talents and energies to contextual appeals which hold considerable potential for destruction of the Black community. It is appropriate that we now consider the more recent phase of the women's movement: programs for women's studies.

Civil Rights in the 1960's and the Emergence of Women's Studies

One of the newest programs within higher education is women's studies which followed the path cleared by Black college students in the 1960's when they demanded representation, participation and relevance in higher education through classes and then programs of Afro-American studies.

The primary focus of women's studies has been upon gender-specific discrimination and the inattention to, as well as the lack of analyses of women's roles in the development of the nation. The first *women's* studies class was taught in the *late 1960's* and was based on the model set by Afro-American Studies. Presenting themselves as "woman as nigger," predominantly White groups of women in higher education spoke of their oppression as analogous to that of the Black American.

In some instances, the initiation of women's studies presented a direct threat to the already established degree-granting programs for Afro-American studies because of the increased demand that was placed on "minority study dollars" that were to be further stretched. The scenario of "minority" competition for limited economic resources is well known. Thus, we can see how in some situations the emergence of women's studies was viewed with serious concern by Black women committed to African American studies and to the philosophy of Black liberation as the means through which sexism and racism would be equally attacked.

Black women in Black studies watched the emergence of women's studies and at the same time heard an appeal by faculty and students for the recruitment to higher education of increased numbers of "minorities," i.e., women and Black faculty. Black women in higher education, well aware of the need for a critical mass of Black faculty, listened to the administrative appeals for "Black faculty and women" and tried to determine where their already scattered energies should be concentrated.

More importantly, Black women in higher education were aware of the more extensive resource pool from which White women faculty could emerge compared to a shrinking pool -- due to decreases in financial aid -- of Black scholars. Already, White women faculty, although very much in the minority, considerably outnumbered Black faculty, both male and female. Even in their oppression, White women have been able to obtain those credentials which make them more readily available when there is a push for "minority" recruitment. It may be documented, for example, that white males in higher education reportedly losing their jobs to Black women are actually losing their jobs to White women.

With few exceptions, women's studies follow in the tradition of the Eurocentric perspective of higher education, only with a gender-specific theme. Most often the curriculum does not include significant numbers of courses, if any, about non-White women. Where such courses are present, the Black female experience is cast into a "traditional" course in which the

Black female/Black male pathology model emerges. In those instances where this traditional literature has been abandoned, and, in particular, where there is some specific curriculum representation of Black women, the perspective which usually dominates is that of the radical feminist and the radical feminist lesbian who certainly present valid issues of oppression, but, who do not represent the primary experiences of the pluralistic majority of Black women.

Moreover, the perspective of most women's studies programs is that Black and White women have suffered a common experience of oppression which is gender-specific. There is a pervasive unwillingness to acknowledge the distinctively *different nature* of oppression for White and non-White women. Seldom is attention given the extent to which White women have benefited from the oppression of Black women and/or have been active participants in racism.

Black Women as Victims of a Trilogy of Oppression

Racism, sexism and economic oppression are so pervasively entwined in America, Black women might reasonably be expected to have difficulty identifying which negative experience is the primary cause of their oppression at any given time. Indeed, most often, these three oppressive forces impact upon Black women simultaneously with a relentlessness that leaves them drained of both creativity and vision. Without a doubt, a by-product of the most minimal resistance to this relentless attack is exhaustion. Our observation has been that most Black women at any given moment will first and foremost report themselves to be tired and exhausted. "Lord, I am weary," is a recurring theme.

In too many instances, what results from this three-pronged attack is a "survival" mentality that can give only limited thought to aggressive strategies and long-term planning. Tragically, one is frequently able to view destructive patterns of escape from the attacks such as: (1) a religious fanaticism which becomes a substitute for personal interactions and gratifying self-giving; (2) a pattern of "other" blaming which allows the victim to suspect the "ill-intentions" of *everyone*; or (3) at the other extreme a self-doubt and self-blame which result in total dependency upon others for validation, in particular, a dependency upon male validation that often allows for extreme abuse, both physical and psychological. In many instances, such abuse is perceived to be their "just due" by Black women thinking themselves worthy of little else. Moreover, because of the limited potential for a long-term monogamous relationship, many women accept abuse in exchange for secure sexual relationships. Clearly, the "victim" mentality emerges from and contributes to the three-pronged attack of racism, sexism and economic exploitation of Black women.

It is appropriate to define these oppressive forces before we consider how Black women have been able to respond:

Racism - a condition of control over the means for both the life chances and lifestyles of the subordinated other through the use of stigma, pejorative treatment, and discrimination resulting in differential opportunities and highly differentiated sharing in the rewards of society. The precondition for racism is the *power* to control and manipulate the major societal forces, and the ability to define for the "other" the requirements for participation. Fundamental to racism is a belief system that places a supremacy focus upon one group over the other. In the western world, this racial supremacy has been translated to mean Anglo-Saxon male.

Sexism - the use by males of the power of gender through both legal and nonlegal means to dominate through pejorative treatment people of the opposite gender (females). Such power is most often the result of superiority attitudes manifested through the rules of society that are both determined and enforced by the control group men. The dictates for sexism may be observed to emerge through physical dominance, through a religious belief system which promotes the view of a divine order which mandates male power, or through the skillful use of sexual politics.

Economic oppression - subjugation and exploitation of the "other" through differential opportunities maintained through discrimination seated in racism. Limited access to the rewards of the system. The earning and purchasing power of groups is limited by those in power through a control over the means for production and distribution of the rewards. This control usually emerges from an internalized system of privilege and hierarchy based upon race and male gender which justifies consolidations and coalitions which block out others. There is, as well, the ability to maintain people control through local, state and federal military. A popular participation in consumerism enhances the power of those in economic control.

Given the fact that race and sex are ascribed characteristics and since in American society these two characteristics relegate non-Whites to a caste group with limited influence and economic opportunity, it might be argued that the African American female is born into a trilogy of oppression from which there are very limited opportunities for escape. Survival under these conditions is at best tenuous. It is small wonder that those Black women who do survive under such conditions, and who also manage to fight back and maintain a positive sense of self, find themselves sanctioned and labeled by three power groups who are: (1) the board members of the White male club, (2) those of the structure who aspire to (top) board membership in the club

18

(other White males), and (3) those who receive some fringe benefits because of gender identity (Black males).

We are all familiar with the denigrating labels which confront the Black woman who strikes out and dares to maintain a valued self; such women are variously viewed to be: domineering, aggressive, probably non-threatening to the man, bad-looking/bad-acting women that no man wants. More recently, they are also presumed to be man-hating homosexuals. A small group of Black women escape from those labels only to find that they must confront other labels which identify them as: (1) harmless types who know their proper place; (2) sexless matronly family heads who contentedly rock on the front porch to the tune of "The Lord Will Provide"; (3) the modern day nanny whose functioning enhances the power of the dominant group; (4) the young survivalist who is allowed to manipulate within limitations under the control of "her man"; (5) the blue collar to white collar educated and trained woman who is legitimized by the power group and allowed to receive limited rewards as long as she is a supporter of the established order; and finally (6) the talented Black woman who entertains us all and is often compromised and non-threatening because of financial co-optation and/or interracial marriage.

These are the most familiar stereotypes used to represent Black women. Such images are presented and reinforced through every means for education and communication within the society; from the all-powerful television, to movies, to radio, to award-winning books praised by culturally selective White critics. Each generation of Black women has grown up with its version of the Beulah, the Sapphire, the tragic semi-precious mulatto, the long-suffering abused survivalist, the so-called bourgeois college woman snob. The tragedy is the extent to which many Black women have internalized these stereotypes and have eventually assumed such roles -- thus, participating in

Stereotypes of black women

a self-fulfilling prophecy as well as the process of victim blaming.

In spite of a long history of the manipulation of these stigmas which enhance the control and power of the major perpetrators of racism, sexism and economic oppression, the majority of Black women have managed to maintain positive self-identities, and to experience some levels of success as mothers, wives, sisters and daughters; as leaders, activists, women working outside of the home; and as women generally contributing to the quality of life within the African American community. Traditional history, and in large measure African American studies and women's studies, have most often excluded any focus upon the experiences of these Black women.

However, more recent socio-historic research evidences positive self-perceptions by Black women in America since the time of the sprinkling of the diaspora on this continent through chattel slavery. Clearly, the various forms of female slave resistance, the anti-racism and anti-sexism activities of Black women's organizations, and their partnership with Black men in the women's organizations, and their partnership with Black men in the struggle against oppression are all evidences of collective positive consciousness among African American women.

Regrettably, many African American women do not know their own history, nor do they know of the cultural linkages between themselves and other women of the African diaspora. African American women of today must learn that they are a part of the continuity between African women and women of the diaspora. They must embrace that heritage with praise and love.

A Brief Look at the Socio-Historic Record

Excellent historical research and Afrocentric sociological studies have more recently extricated the Black woman from obscurity and falsely reported limited roles and replaced these with a more correct view of her dynamic and forceful presence in the struggle against oppression. The socio-historic record is presented in excellent scholarly form by a number of works, including those by Angela Davis, Gerda Lerner, Darlene Clarke Hine, Jeanne Noble, Sharon Harley, Rosalyn Terborg-Penn, LaFrances Rodgers-Rose, Joyce Ladner, Jacquelin Jackson, and Linda Perkins, to name a few women scholars concerned with Black women's issues.

These works report through either historic chronicle or sociological analyses the positive self-perceptions of Black women who, in addition to maintaining responsibilities to family, have devoted presence and talent to the liberation continuum. Of particular importance to us at this time is the extent to which such works highlight the difference in the nature of oppression experienced by Black and White women, and the difference in organizational as well as personal responses to such oppression. As Gerda Lerner, a White woman historian and author of one of the more popular Black women's histories writes:

> ... Black women have always been more conscious of and more handicapped by race oppressions than by sex oppressions. They have been subject to all of the restrictions against blacks and to those against women. In no area of life have they been permitted to attain higher levels of status than White women. Additionally, ever since slavery, they have been sexually exploited by White men through rape or in forced sexual services. These sexual mores, which are characteristic of the relationship of colonializers to the women of the

conquered group, function not only symbolically but actually to fasten the badge of inferiority onto the enslaved group. The black man was degraded by being deprived of the power and the right to protect his women from white men. The black woman was directly degraded by the sexual attack and, more profoundly, by being deprived of a strong black man on whom she could rely for protection.

... Black women have had an ambiguous role in relation to white society. Because they were women, white society has considered them more docile, less than a threat than black men. It has "rewarded" them by allowing -- or forcing -- black women into service in the white family. Black women, ever since slavery, have nursed and raised white children, attended white people in sickness and kept white homes running smoothly. Their intimate contact with white people has made them interpreters and intermediaries of the white culture in the black home. They have consistently had the lowest status in society -- the economic and social -- political status ranking order consisting of white men, white women, black men, black women. Black women's wages, even today, are lowest of all groups.[4]

To the extent that White female leaders and scholars refuse to acknowledge this difference in the nature of the oppressive experiences of Black and White women in America, it is certain that there can never be a viable coalition between African American and Euro-American women. As is evident from these very terms, we are speaking about two historically different cultural orientations. Black women can not negate their Afrocentricity just as White women can not negate their Eurocentricisms.

Status and Color Conflict among Black Women

Much has been written about the patterns of stratification within the ranks of Black womanhood as well as the Black community. Such stratification patterns have primarily emerged as a result of "White owner" validations of "better than" for those of their acknowledged biological paternity. It is most often stated that such "fair skinned women" were privileged by close contact with White owners as house slaves compared to those who were the field slaves during the time of chattel slavery in America. However, when we review the contemporary research about slave women, especially the research by Black women scholars, we learn that for the mulatto female the position as house slave was seldom one of privilege. Those female house slaves served both as beasts of burden, with no lessened physical labor, and, in addition to that role, the mulatto was especially selected for sexual exploitation by White men and their appointed studs. They were "selected" for White male owner profits from prostitution. White males were the initial "pimps" of African American women whose bodies they owned, and whose sexual exploitation was accepted as a part of the master-owner mentality that pervaded.

Moreover, the mulatto female slave was also faced with the wrath of the plantation mistress who was daily forced to confront this symbol of White male (father, husband, son) lust. Atrocities were perpetuated upon Black slave women and, in particular, the female mulatto house slave resulting from the rage and jealousies of White women who often both resented and envied the collective strengths of slave women. It has been suggested, for example, that the ultimate pain of having one's child sold away was a primary threat practiced by White women against their Black slave women.

We know, also, from studies of the plantation records and personal diaries of plantation mistresses, by Angela Davis, Darlene Clark Hine, Kate Willenstein, and others, that the daily abuse as laborer as well as the sexual abuse and exploitation of Black women slaves was most often dismissed or ignored by White women who refused to make a gender association. For example, the White plantation mistress usually avoided making any identification with female slaves as women, for to have used such a term would have been to acknowledge a shared gender relationship by them and the slave women. It is reported that in times of sympathy, plantation mistresses often viewed slave women paternalistically as did White men, referring to them as "poor creatures," "wretched creatures," "the suffering females of their kind." In times of anger and revenge, those same White women referred to Black slave women as "wenches," "libidinous whores," or "apt breeders." Thus, the stratification of slave women by skin color and the so-called privileged position of the "fair skinned" among those same women was imposed upon the slave community.

Skin color divisions among women within the African American community have been promoted because of *dominant other* evaluations of value and worth.[5] Such divisions are ultimately incredulous for no matter how overtly rewarded by the dominant group, no individual Black woman is immune to the darts of oppression for those who step out of their appointed (anointed) roles -- whether that role is based upon skin color, athletic ability, income, education or other factors. That Black women continue to allow unity and sisterhood to be interrupted by divisions based upon color and status is a testimony to the incredible extent to which an oppressed people who do not control the means for their own education are subject to indoctrination which often results in an identification with the oppressor.

The Black woman who is on the lowest economic, status and prestige rung, barely surviving and not knowing from time to time how she will provide for her children or herself, and her Black sister (who because of *relative* opportunity, education or luck has been able to be upwardly mobile within the allowed limitations) are inextricably linked by their common oppression whether it takes the form of the overt daily hassle of the street or the covert sugar-coated arsenic of higher education. The sister struggling to feed her family and the sister of more fortunate economic circumstance (no matter how hostile they may be to each other at one level) know, that on the other level, they have *both* been called "Black bitch" with equal venom. The more pervasive tragedy is that they are seldom aware of their bond -- sisterhood -- other than through the factors of oppression.

> "... The codification of Blackness and femaleness by whites and males is seen in terms of 'thinking like a woman' and 'acting like a nigger' which are based on the premise that there are typically Black and female ways of acting and thinking. Therefore, the most pejorative concept in the white/male world view would be that of thinking and acting like a 'nigger woman.'"[5]

These two groups of Black women who function on different levels of stratification could learn much from each other. They are historically linked to the Motherland and they are linked in the struggle in America to raise whole and decent children; the struggle to maintain meaningful relationships with Black men, etc. At different levels they fight the same battle, which equally exhausts and often destroys them, through different means; however, destruction is destruction.

African American women must reconstruct their supportive linkages, many of which have been severed because of their rejection of each other. This rejection will be increased by a women's movement based upon a strictly gender definition of oppression and for whom the primary participant is middle and upper-middle income women. The division promoted by such a movement could be devastating. It is a division which allows for an additional blow to the often shaky foundations of unity among Black women of a range of hues, and socioeconomic circumstances. Therefore, existing Black women's organizations, whether they be community-based or select small groups, must focus upon the issues which the feminist movement so readily *identifies*, but fails to *embrace* with any *real solutions*: abortion, sexual harassment on the job, rape, childcare, medical abuse, and limited opportunities for education and training -- to name some of the more salient issues.

White feminists who point to a so-called lack of involvement by Black women in women's issues reflect a lack of awareness of the historic role of Black women. Such feminists also fail to realize the extent to which they accept and continue to be influenced by the White male-dominated record of women's history and African American events. Moreover, such persons must realize that historically and contemporarily, African American women have been and are involved in activities which have directly confronted sexism and racism. That resistance has taken them into many dangerous situations in which they have frequently sought, but more often did not receive, the alliance of White feminist advocates.

African slave women were the initiators of feminism in America. It was their struggle for the humanity of womanhood that first made White women aware of White male paternalism which limited their development, but idolized their status. As Paula Giddings reports in her very recent work:

"... The White wife was hoisted on a pedestal so high that she was beyond the sensual reach of her own husband. Black women were consigned to the other end of the scale, as mistresses, whores, or breeders. Thus, in the nineteenth century, Black women's resistance to slavery took on an added dimension. With the diminution of overt rebellion, their resistance became more covert and internalized. The focus of the struggle was no longer against the notion that they were less human,... but that they were different kinds of humans. For women this meant spurning their morally inferior roles of mistresses, whore and breeder -- though under the 'new' slavery they were 'rewarded' for acquiescing in them. It was the factor of reward that made this resistance a fundamentally feminist one, for at its base was a rejection of the notion that they were the master's property. So Black women had a double challenge under the new slavery: They had to resist the property relation (which was different in form, if not in nature, to that of White women) and they had to inculcate the same values into succeeding generations."[6]

Repeatedly, White feminists have been unwilling to acknowledge the extent to which they have participated either overtly or through complicity in the oppression and destruction of Black women. Also, such women have not been willing to admit their privileged position of control over the immediate lives of most *contemporary* Black women. For example, how many White women feminists provide security for their domestics through (1) minimum wages, (2) a retirement plan, (3) sick leave with pay, (4) maternity leave, or (5) a confrontation with their fathers, husbands, sons, brothers and lovers who are the perpetrators of sexual harassment against Black women? White women in the workforce have higher status and most often are in positions of superior power to Black women who have historically been in the workforce in greater numbers and over longer time periods.

Sexual Politics

Contemporary White feminists often attempt to impose upon Black women a definition for Black male/female relationships based upon their perspectives which identify all men as the enemy. Such women point to examples of Black male abuse of Black women and call to Black women for disassociation with Black males as if such men were in the same positions of power as White males.

Clearly, sexism and abuse of Black women by Black men can be observed and may be documented to exist as a serious problem within the Black community. However, the Black community vis-a-vis Black women, must define their own problems and the means through which those problems might best be resolved with minimal injury to all.

Historically, Black women have functioned in different relationships to Black men than have White women with White men. More importantly, when we view sexual politics as expressed through rape and other violent crimes, a point of orientation must be the extent to which Black on Black crime results most ostensibly from White on Black crime

Some Black feminists have observed that rape is an emotional issue which emerges as a concern for White women primarily as an emotional attention-getting issue. They point out that the White woman's primary victimization by White men is in less violent forms, such as economic and political sexual politics. In particular, when calling attention to abuses of Black women by Black men, White feminists point to the Black man as the potential rapist of White women. A key issue for Black women must also be the extent to which the White female/ male focus upon the Black male as rapist is a focus upon a presumed Black female promiscuity. As Angela Davis reports, "the mythical rapist implies the mythical whore."

"... It cannot be denied that Brownmiller's book, *Against Our Will: Men, Women and Rape*, is a pioneering scholarly contribution to the contemporary literature on rape. Yet many of her arguments are unfortunately pervaded with racist ideas. Characteristic of that perspective is her reinterpretation of the 1955 lynching of fourteen-year-old Emmett Till. After this young boy had whistled at a white woman in Mississippi, his maimed body was found at the bottom of the Tallahatchie River. 'Till's action,' said Brownmiller, 'was more than a kid's brash prank.'

While Brownmiller deplores the sadistic punishment inflicted on Emmett Till, the Black youth emerges, nonetheless, as a guilty sexist -- almost as guilty as his white racist murderers. After all, she argues, both Till and his murderers were exclusively concerned about their rights of possession over women."[7]

Davis continues by citing the work by Jean MacKeller:

"... According to Jean MacKeller,... (*Rape: The Bait and the Trap*) 'Blacks raised in the hard life of the ghetto learn that they can get what they want only by seizing it. Violence is the rule in the game for survival. Women are fair prey: to obtain a woman one subdues her.'

... MacKeller has been so completely mesmerized by racist propaganda that she makes the unabashed claim that 90 percent of all reported rapes in the United States are committed by Black men. Inasmuch as the FBI's corresponding figure is 47 percent; it is difficult to believe that MacKeller's statement is not an intentional provocation."[8]

If these discussions which link rape (for which the Black woman is most often the victim) as a primary preoccupation by

Black men and with a so-called promiscuity of Black women (a link which emerged as a justification for White male rape of slave women), even more devastating are the works by Black male writers of the 1960's, such as Claude Brown's *Manchild* or Calvin Hernton who support myths established by White males. As Davis critiques:

"... 'the Negro woman during slavery began to develop a depreciatory concept of herself, not only as a female but as a human being as well.' According to Hernton's analysis, 'after experiencing the ceaseless sexual immorality of the white south,' ... the Negro woman became 'promiscuous and loose,' and could be 'had for the taking. Indeed, she came to look upon herself as the South viewed and treated her, for she had no other morality by which to shape her womanhood.'

Hernton's analysis never penetrates the ideological veil which has resulted in the minimizing of the sexual outrages constantly committed against black women. He falls into the trap of blaming the victim for the savage punishment she has historically been forced to endure."[9]

When Black women have worked throughout history to manifest what Davis calls "a collective consciousness of their sexual victimization," they have labored alone in their appeal before receiving support by White women. One must move into historically recent times, for example, before we find Jessie Daniel Ames and the Association for Southern Women for the Prevention of Lynching. They worked against lynchings purported to be in defense of White women victims of Black male rape. Again, as Davis reports:

"One of the major weaknesses of Susan Brownmiller's study on rape is its absolute disregard of Black women's pioneering efforts in the anti-lynching movement. While

Brownmiller rightfully praises Jessie Daniel Ames and the Association of Southern Women, she makes not so much as a passing mention of Ida B. Wells, Mary Church Terrell or Mary Talbert and the Anti-Lynching Crusaders."[10]

If one is lacking a clear understanding of the relative value placed upon Black women versus White women as violence victims, one need only consider these facts reported by Gloria Joseph:

"Rape is America's fastest-growing violent crime. Black women are eighteen times more likely to be rape victims than are White women... No White male in the history of this country was ever given the death penalty for raping Black women."[11]

Black men who rape Black women are given lighter sentences (if sentenced at all) compared to sentences for the rape of White women. The victim of the Black male rapist is overwhelmingly the Black female. The rate of Black female rape by White males is almost three times higher than the rate of White female rape by Black males. That the dominant society (White male/female) has internalized the value association of White as good and Black as bad appears to be supported by the data reporting crime and punishment by race.

The homicide rate for Black women is superceded only by the homicide rate for Black men. Without a doubt, varying degrees of violence are a part of the life of large numbers of Black women. While much publicity is given to the disproportionate number of Black males in the nation's prisons, limited attention is given to the fact that 48% of the women's prison population is Black. Little research has been conducted to determine why this Black female prison population is so high. It is reasonable to speculate that Black women (like Black men) often find themselves swept up in life situations that are so desperate that violence appears to be the easiest if not the only avenue for a statement of self-hood, or for the resolution of a threat crisis.

To combat these devastating and self-destructive situations within the African American community, the historic alliance between Black men and Black women, politically and socially as defenders, developers and lovers of each other must be strengthened, and in many instances completely reestablished. The gender divisions which the contemporary White feminist movement could promote among Black women would be counter-productive to this vital unifying effort. To be respected by others and in order to be in a workable coalition posture, an oppressed people must first and foremost seek to address their own personal/internal issues.

Economic Inequality by Race and Sex

The stratification patterns of economic inequality are well known. In 1980 the median earnings for full-time White women workers was $11,703 compared to $19,720 for White men or an income gap of approximately 59%. The income gap between Black women and Black men has narrowed over the years; however, the true indicator of economic viability is obtained only when median income by race is compared to that of White men. As the data indicate, the income gaps between Black and White women must be viewed in terms of part-time and full-time working women. The highest national rate of unemployment is among young Black women. Single parent White women are more likely to be employed than Black women.

Even when Black professional women held higher educational levels than Black men, Black men held higher status and higher paying professional jobs. This data is one of the clearest indications of the duality of the attack by sexism and racism upon Black female occupational status and income. Moreover, although Black women have experienced upward occupational mobility, the shift has been from low-status domestic work into lower level clerical work and managerial categories. Compared to Black men, Black women continue to predominate in service work categories and low pay "white collar" occupations.

Married Black women earn 54% of their husband's earnings. This figure indicates the inequality in earning between Black women and men even though both experience racial discrimination in the employment arena. Non-working Black wives are a majority part of the severely "impoverished class," compared to non-working White wives who are part of the "advantaged class."

Data from the census as presented by the Urban League illustrate the Black female/male/White female/male economic relationships.[12]

Although the primary focus of this work is on African American women, the coalition schema and the accompanying power diagrams underscore the common position of oppression shared by American women of color. In a report which highlights the income and occupational differences between White and non-White women, Phyllis Palmer makes the following observations:

"... Although white women are still slightly less likely than women of color to be employed full-time, this figure is also converging. In 1979, 50.4% of white women were in the labor force, and 67% of these, 37,210,000 were employed full-time. Of the 52.5% of

Black women in the labor market, 68% of these, 4,899,999, were employed full-time. And of the 47.3% of Hispanic women in the labor force, 71% of these, 1,859,000, were employed full-time. Another major difference is the likelihood of facing unemployment, and the rates are substantially higher for women of color than for white women. In 1980, when white women had an average rate of 5.6% unemployment, Black women averaged 11.8%, and Spanish origin women averaged 9.6%, running to a high 12.6% among Puerto Rican women. Indeed, one of the ironies of female impoverishment is that the higher the proportion of female-headed household (and therefore the greater the need for female income), the higher the proportion of unemployment.

Finally, a major factor in the differences in women's lives is the occupation within which they find employment. Just as social scientists studying women's low pay relative to men have recognized that the major explanation for the pay differential is that women work in different (and less well-paid) jobs than men do, so white women and various women of color are not proportionally distributed across all occupations, or even across female-dominated ones... service work is still the predominant category for Black women, as it is also for Native American women. Mexican and Puerto Rican women are heavily weighted in the operative category, although this category is second for both of them to clerical work... Much of white women's relative advantage comes from their heavy representation in clerical and in professional-managerial work. Even though they are in the latter category primarily as nurses and schoolteachers, these women's occupations that are low-paid relative to men are high-paid relative to those in which large proportions of women of color find employment."[13]

The impact of this dilemma on the respective communities of women of color is clearly evidenced by Palmer who concludes:

"...it is ironic that women's contribution to family income increases as family income decreases. As Carolyn Shaw Bell has shown in an important study, the lower the family income, the larger is the percentage brought in by women members of the family. This is a reminder that women's economic improvement must proceed on two fronts: raising the incomes women receive relative to me, and raising the incomes men of color and all women receive relative to white men."[14]

Black Women's Organized Efforts Against Racism and Sexism

Historically, as well as today, Black women have worked through their own organizations to eliminate racism and sexism. Because of racism from within the White women's organizations and more recently because such organizations have failed to *seriously* address the primary issue of concern to them, Black women have not joined in a partnership with White women. Reporting the history of racism within women's movements and the emerging formation of separate Black women's organizations, Rosalyn Terborg-Penn writes:

"...Discrimination against Afro-American women reformers was the rule rather than the exception within the woman's rights movement from the 1830's to 1920. ...the prevailing historiography as well as the popular view of the feminist movements of the nineteenth and twentieth centuries is that white women welcomed black women into the cause. Influenced by the rhetoric of female solidarity expressed by white feminists, recent histories of the woman's rights movement in the United States have concluded that because of disinterest, *only a very few black women responded to the call.* When, however, one looks behind the rhetoric to examine the actual experiences of black women who attempted to join the organizations of white feminists, it becomes clear that the recent assumptions by historians need to be revised.

... Discrimination against black women in abolitionist societies organized by white women appears ironic when one considers that white women complained of discrimination by men.

... Abhorrence of slavery was no guarantee that white reformers would accept the Afro-American on equal terms. In 1835, for example, Afro-American women began attending the Massachusetts Female Anti-Slavery Society at Fall River, causing such a controversy among the white members that dissolution of the group nearly resulted. Furthermore, Sarah Douglass, an active member of the Quakers, a group known for their participation in the antislavery cause, expressed her feelings of alienation from white church members because they discriminated against her... Degree of skin color was also a factor in determining the acceptability of blacks by whites. *Light-skinned Afro-American women appear to have been preferred in white female groups.* Benjamin Quarles notes comments made to this effect by a member of the Boston Female Anti-Slavery Society about the fair-skinned Susan Paul. Because of this antiblack prejudice, Afro-American women may have avoided participation in groups like the National Convention of Female Anti-Slavery Societies."[15]

Underscoring the extent to which feminism among White women can be linked to the concept of White supremacy, Robert Allen reports:

"Middle-class suffragists were appalled at the thought of class struggle and accepted the basic structure of their society: they simply wanted to participate more fully in its affairs. They sought, therefore, to show that the woman's vote would benefit the existing social structure and that the reforms women would enact would not alter the basic social relations.

In an era when the Anglo-Saxon population feared the voting strength of immigrants and the nonwhite peoples, they tried to show that woman suffrage would increase -- or at least not limit -- Ango-Saxon majority... Nationally (the woman's movement) was connected to the Progressive movement and shared with that movement the belief in white supremacy.

With the exception of their demands for equal rights, feminists and other female reformers shared the same views as the men of their class.

... Suffrage leaders for the most part agreed with the prevailing racism which blamed blacks for the failure of Reconstruction and their disenfranchisment, and sought to win women's suffrage through demonstrating their allegiance to white supremacy. Feminism came to mean predominantly (although not solely) the fight of white women to be included in the rights and privileges of a racist society."[16]

Clearly, there has been a long record of exclusion of Black women from most White female organizations in behalf of women's rights. As Tuborg-Penn reports, the record of the experience of women, such as Frances Harper, Josephine Ruffin, Mary Terrell, Ida B. Wells, is a record of discrimination against Black women by White feminist groups.

Historian Cynthia Morton chronicles the extent to which Black women confronted sexism by Black men, managed dual roles as women and activists as well as the extent to which Black women leaders marched across divisions of economic class in behalf of both female and community issues. Morton reports:

"Josephine Turpin Washington, a Richmond teacher and author, stated that many people believed that 'the true woman takes her place by the side of man as his companion, his co-worker, his helpmate, his equal, but she never forgets that she is a woman and not a man.' This definition of the role of the black woman was shared in part, or totally, by a number of black men and women. Rosetta Douglass Sprague, the oldest child of Frederick Douglass, felt that educated black women could be most effective in the home. She saw their role as being the same as that of other women. In addition, she believed that black women could assist their towns in developing aid societies for the maintenance of kindergartens of the Women's League, ... a teacher for twenty-five years throughout the South, stated that the educated black woman had to be in front of the crusade against ignorance, vice, and crime. To do this, she had to go where the blacks were living. In further defining the relationship between men and women, Bowser stated: "Men are what the women make them. Above all, the thought must be impressed indelibly upon the hearts and consciences of the youth that men can be no better than the women.'"[17]

It must be remembered, however, that "feminist resistance" by Black women can be observed from the earliest days of the bondaged mass introduction of Africans onto the American shores (it is noted that there is a documented African presence on the American continent long before its "discovery" by Columbus). The resistance of slave women included armed rebellion not often reported. The potential for armed rebellion among Black women followed the same range of probability as for Black men. Both Black men and women have embraced any means possible in the fight against oppression.

> "If Black women bore the terrible burden of equality in oppression, if they enjoyed equality with their men in their domestic environment, then they also asserted their equality aggressively in challenging the inhumane institution of slavery. They resisted the sexual assaults of white men, defended their families and participated in work stoppages and revolts... they poisoned their masters, committed other acts of sabotage and, like their men, joined maroon communities and frequently fled northward to freedom. From the numerous accounts of the violent repression overseers inflicted on women, it must be inferred that she who passively accepted her lot as a slave was the exception rather than the rule."[18]

Paula Giddings has also reported about the early "feminist efforts" by Black slave women:

> "... As both the race and feminist issues intensified in the 1840's and 1850's, it was inevitable that Black and White women abolitionists would come to a parting of the ways. The parting was due not only to White racism, but also to the primacy of race or sex as issues in their respective struggles. All Black women abolitionists (and most of the leading Black male abolitionists) were feminists. But when it came to the question of priorities, race, for most of them, came first... for Black women it was the issue of race that sparked their feminism.

> There was something else, too. As Sojourner Truth's message implied, Black women had already proven their inherent strengths -- both physical and psychological. They had undergone a baptism of fire and emerged intact. Therefore, their convictions concerning the rights

of women were deeply rooted in experience as well as theory."[19]

It would appear that the present feminist organization ideology continues to ignore deep-seated racism. In a discussion about this matter, Patsy Fulcher reported that in 1977 the National Organization of Women (NOW) had no minority women on its board and that that condition continued in the 1983 election. Fulcher highlighted the fact that such conditions make a statement to Black women and suggest that the leadership efforts and abilities of Black women will continue to be ignored or unrewarded. As a result of the negation of Black women leadership by NOW, there was formed the National Women's Political Caucus which questioned the viability of even issue-specific cosponsorship between the NWPC and NOW.[20]

In a similar manner, in 1977 at the Houston Conference of the International Woman's Year, a Black woman's action plan emerged because of such women's awareness of the need to address problems which were not a vital part of the White woman dominated IWY Conference. Pointing to the significantly different historical and cultural backgrounds and experiences of Black women and White women, the framers of the Black Women's Action Plan wrote:

... Black women have endured a dual burden of racism and sexism... rejection and subjugation based upon race and color... have had the effect of maintaining special privileges and power for the benefit of the white majority. Further, they have reinforced each other... Generally, this involvement in the economic realm, resulted in a sharp contrast between the social-economic relations of the majority female vis-a-vis the majority male, and the black female vis-a-vis the black male. The fact that black women have a different past, a different present, and because of institutionalized racism, a different future from that of white women, it is doubtful that anyone else in the United States can or should speak for them. Therefore, black women members of IWY assume the responsibility of their own interpretation of women's mission, believing that it is only on the basis of sound, historically correct analysis that women of the minority and the majority in the nation may organize effectively around their specific (concerns) as women and press for not only women's rights, but more importantly, human rights.

... Moreover, as black women informed by our past we must eschew a view of the women's struggle which takes as its basic assumption opposition to men, as distinguished from organizing around the principle of opposition to the white, male power-structure's perpetuation of exploitation, subjugation, inequality and limited opportunities based upon sex or race. In this regard one permanent issue of a vigilant, progressive women's movement must be, "who shall, in what manner, frame the issues to which women are to address themselves in a society whose majority is culturally conditioned to operate upon the basis of racist and sexist assumptions."[21]

Joyce Ladner further describes the issue:

... Black women do not perceive their enemy to be Black men, but rather the enemy is considered to be the oppressive forces in the larger society which subjugate Black *men, women and children* . A preoccupation with the equalization of roles between Black men and women is almost irrelevant when one places it within the context of total priorities related to the survival of the race.[22]

The Black Women's Action Plan proposed at the IWY Conference called for attention to the pertinent issues of Black women, listed to be:

Education...recognizing the political, socio-economic and human costs of discriminatory education and educational opportunities limited by racism and sexism...

Employment...unemployment and under-utilization of black females as a resource in the labor force at all levels, policies and positions which either focus upon employment of women at the expense of black men or identify black women as threats to qualified non-minority (persons)...

Political Participation...believing that reform must be pressed through the political system...

Socially Progressive Services...and uncompromising belief that our concern must be for the improvement of the quality of human life in order that full human development may be fostered...

Statutory and Constitutional Law...the federal government must be called on to use its full power to protect and support...human rights...

Housing...the national goal of a decent, safe and sanitary home in a suitable living environment for every American family...especially for the families of black and other minority women who have been denied decent housing by reason of discrimination based upon race and sex...[23]

White feminists concern about a place in the structure may be contrasted with non-White women's concerns about structured inequality. This is dramatically underscored by Veronica Collazzo and Sharon Parker who reported to the National Institute for Women of Color:

... While the pro-ERA leadership learned by its mistakes and ultimately achieved a significant political 'machine' fueled by the energy, dedication and resources of thousands of women and men, the 'machine' could have been even stronger if more women of color and ethnic communities had become involved. A very significant strategical omission, which went largely unnoticed by the mass media, was the failure of the ERA campaign to address and to incorporate the insight and perspective of women of color.

... Despite the media blitz of the final weeks, the faces and voices exhorting Americans to support the ERA were overwhelmingly those of white Americans... a woman of color was never the sole or primary speaker for the ERA at a highly visible and public event... How is it then that an issue so critically important to all women in this country, as the proponents regularly pointed out, did not include a proportional representation of women of color among its primary leaders and spokeswomen?

... The crux of the question, however, lies more in an analysis of leadership within American society and the women's movement... the typical American leader, in most circumstances, is contrary to the concept of leadership within many minority cultures.

... Personal ambition among peoples who share a history of neglect and oppression is often suppressed when it does not promise greater benefit for the group. As a result, it is not uncommon for minority cultural values to be obscured by the predominant competitive approach to leadership."[24]

Parker and Collazo report the aggressive and influential requirements for leadership in America as characteristic of the leadership sought by the ERA effort. They also reported that non-White women were not able to compete with the leisure time of majority women who were able to leave family to meet the ERA demands. They called attention to the cultural patterns and socio-economic factors which prevented a non-White women's leadership. In their concluding discussion, Collazzo and Parker report the extent to which concerns by non-White women were consistently swept into the background. They report:

"... Locked in the bosom of sisterhood, we found ourselves cherished and nurtured to a point. The point was a limitation on the extent to which racial discrimination could overshadow sexual discrimination. As long as we faithfully represented the cause of women, we were encouraged to speak for women's issues. Mention could even be made of our special plight as women of color as long as it served to reinforce, not override, the abject picture of women as victims of discrimination.

... Just short of the ratification deadline, an effort was made to include 'more representative' faces among those extolling the virtues of the ERA. Women of color were recruited who could speak on the issue of the ERA without confusing the public with the correlation between sexism and racism... However, the strategy to persuade people of color failed because the ERA leadership remained devoid of a critical factor -- the perception of leadership by and among people of color.

... Women of color could have advised the ERA leadership that we regard individuals as leaders only when they have gained our respect, trust and support. It is not enough to simply identify with their color, race, community or constituency. The issue, and the leader, must be owned and accepted by the community (underlined here for emphasis) before support can be mobilized in any direction.

Discounting people of color in the belief that we were a marginal factor -- an insignificant minority -- was indeed a crucial strategical error with predictable results."[25]

Parker and Collazo who are respectively Chair and founder and Vice Chairpersons of the NIWC Board of Directors conclude:

"... The double jeopardy suffered by women of color who are subjected to racist as well as sexist treatment under the law makes the ratification of the ERA a particularly meaningful and relevant issue within the current political environment. Women of color stood to gain increased protection against discriminatory statutes yet suffered the most severe setback with the defeat of the ERA. We must not allow others to develop the strategy and to assume the leadership in struggles to achieve social justice..."[26]

The Present and Future Struggle: A Typology of Attitudes

Thus far, I have presented a summary of the socio-historic and socio-political factors which support the contention that there is need for serious question about the viability of a Black/White woman's coalition in the social movement popularly known as women's liberation. Although many of the goals presented by the movement are of vital importance to the life style and life chances of Black women, it would appear that when the opportunity to achieve such goals have been sought by Black women, they have most often found White women among their strongest adversaries.

In particular, I have called attention to the dramatic difference from White women in the nature of the oppression of Black women who have confronted sexism, racism and economic oppression. The dehumanization experienced by American women of the African diaspora and other women of non-White cultures remains unparalleled by American White women. To presume a simplistic common enemy (all men) as an obvious basis for coalition is to deny American non-White women their hard fought struggle against Anglo-American cultural imperialism as well as the experiences of sexism, racism and economic oppression.

In the presentation of a summary of activities by Black women against oppression I have indicated the collective nature of their self-definitions which have been and continue to be "we" opposed to the "I" of European cultures. If I were to summarize the difference in the message which emanates from Black/White women it would be that White women send a message that states: "I have worked hard. I have been oppressed. It is past the time when I should take my rightful place in the structure beside you." The message which emerges from the Black woman is: "...the structure is wrong. It works against us as Black people." Viewing the structure to consistently say "get back, you're black" African American women have clearly identified racism as the primary evil to attack.

A content analysis of the literature reporting attitudes by Black women about the White feminist movement allows for the development of a typology which clearly illustrates the extent to which the African American women continues to express a collective concern about racism as a priority issue. The Gordon Typology is still emerging and may vary as additional data are available. My most recent research about Black Women in a Typical Town (forthcoming) will present data reflecting African American women's views about a range of contemporary issues. A first level evaluation of those data indicates attitudes about the women's movement to be consistent with the typology presented. The typology may be summarized to support the following perspectives:

1. Racism should be the primary target for African Americans.

2. It is difficult to wage a battle on two fronts with limited resources, and the issue of race is primary.

3. Black women do not want to compartmentalize themselves into segments of race vs. gender.

4. In large measure, Black male sexism emerges from racism which prevents/limits Black male personal and professional development. Facing a lack of power in a society which rewards men for power, the Black male participates in misdirected hostilities against women and others in the community. In large measure, rape and domestic violence will be diminished when Black men have the opportunity for positive means for definitions of "manhood." Black on Black crime results primarily from White on Black crime.

5. Black liberation represents freedom from sexism and racism and embraces a Black female/male co-partnership in struggle and love. To the extent that the movement fails in this focus, Black women and men who are enlightened must actively work to teach and influence others; thereby, maintaining the Black struggle focus.

6. Black female participation in White feminist movements presumes that Black males hold equal power with White males by defining all men as the enemy.

7. Although sexism has been practiced by males in the various Civil Rights movements, the extent to which it existed and restricted/subjugated Black women has been exaggerated.

Table 1

Gordon's
Typology of Black Women's Attitudes
About the Women's Liberation Movement

Triple Jeopardy Issue

Racism/Sexism/Economics
vs.
Sexism/Economics

a. The movement lacks a clear focus upon the complexity of the oppressed condition of Black women.

b. Black women are victims of racism, sexism and economic exploitation.

c. The relative degree of economic exploitation varies drastically for Black and White women.

d. White women have benefitted from and participated in the oppressions of Black women.

e. White women continue to behave in manners which differ / do not reflect concerns about Black women.

f. The movement fails to state clearly that the system is wrong; what it does communicate is that White women want to be a part of the system. They seek power, not change.

Gordon's Typology (cont)

Socioracial and Sociocultural Factors

Counterproductive Use
of Human Resources

a. The movement calls upon Black women to define themselves apart from the total Black experience.

b. The Black women's focus has been / is upon the needs of the total community.

The movement threatens the unity needed for Black liberation

a. Limited talents and resources will be drained away from the community.

b. Black liberation would end sexism as well as racism.

Countercultural Focus
of the Movement

a. The movement calls upon Black women to define themselves apart from the total Black experience.

b. The Black women's focus has been / is upon the needs of the total community.

The movement threatens the unity needed for Black liberation

a. The movement threatens the more egalitarian Black male/female relationships.

b. There is the potential for a reduction in the probability of a long-term monogamous relationship.

c. The movement appeals to women who want to be men - radical feminist lesbians or manhaters.

d. Anglo-community involvement encourages self, self-group hostility; holds potential for negative values of self by Black women.

Gordon's Typology (cont)

Historic Record and
Matter of Trust
Historic Record

a. There is no history of a common oppression of Black and White women.

b. The relative degree of economic exploitation varies drastically for Black and White women.

c. White women have benefitted from and participated in the oppressions of Black women.

Socioeconomic/
Caste Issues

Anti-Capitalist
Sentiment

a. The movement is another indication of the exploitive nature of capitalism which requires an underclass.

b. The movement is another smokescreen. "Sexism" is a coverup of the real issues of economic exploitation of the many by the few.

c. White feminists have not communicated with poor white women who see the movement as unrelated to their needs.

d. The White feminist group represents the interests of a select group of women who have the leisure to develop organizational efforts primarily in their own behalf.

Major Issues of Concern to Black Women

In a separate book, *AFRICAN AMERICAN WOMEN: Contemporary Issues*, a detailed presentation will be made about the perceptions of self and role as identified by a random sample study of Black Women in a typical town. The most immediate information from that study which will be of interest to readers of this book is the rank order of frequency of identification of certain critical issues which "must be of concern to Black Women." The ranking is based upon a content analysis of the responses of 101 Black women in Muncie, Indiana.

As may be observed, the issues identified speak to the dynamics of racism; that is, the conditions of the Black community resulting from a historic and contemporary subordinate position of Blacks in America. Whereas many of the issues identified to be of critical concern to Black women may also be identified by the White dominated Women's movement as issues of concern to all women, the responses by Black women contain a clear and unquestioned focus on those issues as they impact upon the Black community and as they impact uniquely upon Black women.

In the identification of the categories reported, because of the sample size, some collapse of categories was made; that is, health and housing include references made to crime, drugs and rape as they impact upon the mental and physical health of the community. Only one reference was made to teen pregnancy (it should be noted that at the time of the study this issue had not received the media blitz of the more recent year), and that reference was with respect to the need for sex education to prevent teen pregnancy.

Table 2

Major Issues of Concern to Black Women

The issues are in rank order:

1. **Education**

   quality education for children
   adult education for jobs, better life,
        community service
   sex education for teens

2. **Employment**

   availability of jobs
   economic security
   career opportunities
   equal opportunities for jobs and
        income for Blacks and Whites

3. **Family, Home, Motherhood**

   needs of the family
   to be a good mother
   demands of work and family
   needs of children and youth
   needs of the elderly
   male companionship

Table 2

Major Issues of Concern to Black Women (cont)

4. **Housing, Health, Crime**

    quality housing
    housing for the elderly
    focus upon physical and mental health
    general health care
    crime, drugs, rape

5. **Perceptions of Self and Role:**

    positive views about the self as a
        Black Woman
    sexism - lack of respect for Black
        women
    need for personal fulfillment

6. **Leadership:**

    greater civic participation
    need for Black women to seek elected
        office
    need for attention to the conditions of
        the race
    need for Black leadership to provide
        positive role models

7. **Women's Liberation:**

    concern with same issues as those of
        White women
    need for ERA

Of particular importance is an area which receives limited attention by the traditional literature; the Black woman's definition of self. As has been repeatedly presented by this author in other papers and publications, the affirmation of positive selfhood is increasingly of concern to Black women who believe that they suffer from a lack of recognition of their historic role. It is not surprising, therefore, to find this category ranking 4th in frequency of concern in a grouping which identifies 7 primary categories identified from the subject responses.

It should be clearly stated that the goals outlined by the women's liberation movement and the benefits which would be provided by ERA legislation are vital to women of color. The discussion presented by this work should not be viewed in any way to suggest that non-White women have not clearly identified such goals, which include equal pay for equal work; adequate day care for working mothers; freedom from sexual harassment on the job; equal access to training programs for occupational and professional advancement, among others. Clearly, also the protection which the ERA would provide is important to women of color because of their status by race/ethnic and gender.

What I have attempted to emphasize is that (1) African American women have endured abject deprivation while White women have experienced relative deprivation; (2) African American women have been victims of a racism which defined them as less-than human, whereas White women have been defined as having limitations or unique roles appropriate to their gender within the human species; (3) African American women are in a partnership struggle with Black men for the emancipation of their communities and for the expansion of the life chances and life styles of Black youth, while White women enjoy many of the socio-economic benefits which emerge from the power grip of the White male club; (4) African American women have been and continue to be victims of racism by White women. They are the persons with the least power in the proposed coalition. They must be concerned about their potential for the promised rewards. It is maintained that there is limited, if any, convincing evidence from the past or the contemporary women's movement which suggests that this message has been both heard and understood by the majority of the White women participants and leaders in the organized feminist movement.

Directions for Change in Black Male/Female Relationships

The primary concern of this paper has been the African American woman, feminism and Black liberation. However, such a consideration could not conclude without some specific attention to sexism by Black men as it impacts upon the lives of Black women. Appropriately, we must identify some positive actions which can be undertaken by each individual in the resolution of sexism in the Black community and in behalf of the accomplishment of a Black liberation that places equal focus upon sexism and economic and cultural oppression. The following observations/actions represent a first place where everyone could begin:

1. Black women in the mothering role who most often have the responsibility for the socialization of boys and girls must act in behalf of changed sex role attitudes. The Black woman who complains about sexist Black men may often be heard, in the very next breath, to brag about the "sexual prowess" of her son who "has all of the women." These inconsistencies in attitudes about appropriate male behavior communicate unclear

messages to young male and female children and suggest that Black women believe that sexual exploitation or abuse is permissible as long as the victim is someone else.

2. Men must increasingly participate in the earliest care and socialization of children. Such egalitarian and interchangeable home sex role socialization could help young children develop an important reference for self definitions and could lessen the attraction of violence as a solution to sex role conflict. Increased participation in the nurturing role without fear of a loss of "manhood" must become the standard for African American men who view Black women as their true co-partners in the liberation struggle. Enlightened/conscious men must be the primary communicators of this philosophy and behavior to sexist men who would not listen to women until such time as those men are able to communicate with women in a non-defensive manner.

3. At a time when there are tremendous social and economic pressures upon a growing number of female single parent homes, Black men, through the range of augmented male family roles practiced historically in the Black community must provide positive images for young men and women who too often seek identity from the stereotypic images presented in the media.

4. Needless to say, Black men and women who are addressing sexism must clearly understand their definitions of selfhood and their relationships to each other. Each must evaluate both the nature and the quality of given relationships to determine the extent to which, if any, unfair impositions in the various forms of "sexual politics" might be taking place.

5. Realizing the vulnerability the conditions a pervasive racism imposes, African American men and women must extend, sometimes painfully, their ability and willingness

56

to take chances, to trust each other and reveal their individual fragility. Emphasis must be upon the recognition of their balanced strengths. Only that balanced strength can sustain each individual in the struggle. That balanced strength has been a key to success in the past. It must be reestablished for a victory in the present.

Conclusion

Black women continue to insist that their own emancipation cannot be separated from the emancipation of the total African American community. Primarily, such women view themselves to be co-partners with Black men in the struggle against oppression by defining liberation to include freedom from all forms of oppression, including sexism. Strategies for attack upon sexism and racism will be developed and directed by Black women and men who best understand the conditions of their community. It is, therefore, vital that programs and dialogue with the community cut across divisions of class and color although a utopian non-stratified society is not prophesied.

Although racism, sexism and economic exploitation have often drained the vital energies of African American women, there is a historic kinship network which extends beyond their immediate family and community. If there is a central theme which emerges from this work, it is the pride, sense of community and resilience of Black women who have never been content to simply survive, and who have fought at all levels, in all situations and by all means against the enslavement of their bodies, their minds and their communities.

In questioning the viability of Black/White women coalitions, we have concluded that only short-term, issue-specific coalitions are viable. However, even these forms of linkages will result in serious personal surrender by Black women who do not seek historic self-definitions. The call to renewed energies echoes from Zenobia to Tubman; from Hatshepsut to Bethune; from the Ethiopian Judith of Fire to Mary Church Terrell; to you and me.

> ...Tossed by whirlwinds of decision
> I have grasped for one anchor or the other
> choosing as if from separate parts
> seeking the order of my world.
> There was no rest, no peace, no harmony,
> my source was denied.
> Out of the conflict of choice
> after the ENLIGHTENMENT
> order stamped me a triune life
> the trilogy of my personal self
> AFRICAN/AMERICAN/WOMAN

> Satiafa
> 1983

NOTES

1. For research about racism and color symbolism, see: "Religion, Color and Race in American Society," an unpublished dissertation by James Everage, University of Virginia, Charlottesville, Virginia, May 1984.

2. For perspectives presented by non-White women, the reader may wish to see: "Black Women and International Liberation Movements," in *Black Women and Liberation Movements* edited by Virginia A. Blandford. The Institute for the Arts and Humanities, PO Box 723, Howard University, Washington, D.C., 20059.

3. Blalock, Hubert M. *Race and Ethnic Relations.* New Jersey, Prentice Hall, 1982 pp. 109 & 112. For a primary reference and excellent discussion of coalition, see also: Caplow, Theodore. *Two Against One: Coalitions in Triads.* Englewood Cliffs, New Jersey, Prentice-Hall, 1968.

4. Lerner, Gerda. *Black Women in White America.* New York, Vintage Books, 1974, Preface.

5. This discussion is supported by a number of works, including: *The Slave Community* by John Blassingame, *Black Women in White America* by Gerda Lerner, *The Black Community* by James Blackwell, *Slavery and Race Relations in the Americas* by H. Hoetnick.

6. Hull, Gloria T., et al. *All the Women are White, All the Blacks are Men, but Some of Us are Brave: Black Women's Studies.* New York, The Feminist Press, 1982, p. 178.

7. Giddings, Paula. *When and Where I Enter ... The Impact of Black Women on Race and Sex in America.* New York, William Morrow & Co. 1984, p. 43.

8. Davis, Angela. *Women, Race and Class.* New York, Random House, 1981, Chapters 1 & 2.

9. Davis, Angela. Ibid, Chapter 11.

10. Davis, Angela. Ibid.

11. Joseph, Gloria I. and Jill Lewis. *Common Differences.* New York, 1981, pp. 27, 38-39, 278-279.

12. "Economic Policies and Black Progress: Myths and Realities." by Robert Hill. The National Urban League, Washington, D.C., pp. 104, 107, 113, 123.

13. "Economic Facts on Women of Color." A paper prepared for the National Institute for Women of Color, Washington, D.C.

14. Ibid.

15. "Discrimination Against Afro-American Women in the Woman's Movement, 1830-1920." by Rosalyn Terborg-Penn. In *The Afro-American Woman.* Port Washington, New York, 1978, Chapter 2.

16. Allen, Robert. *Reluctant Reformers: Racism and Social Reform Movements in the United States.* Washington, D.C., Howard University Press, 1983, Chapter V.

17. "The Black Woman's Struggle for Equality in the South 1895-1925." by Cynthia Morton. In *The Afro-American Woman.* Port Washington, New York, 1989, Chapter 4.

18. Davis, Angela. op. cit.

19. Giddings, Paula. op. cit.

20. "Black Women in the Women's Movement." Patsy Fulcher, et. al., Washington, D.C., National Public Radio, Horizon Series, HO-800207.01/01-C, 1980. (cassette)

21. "Black Women's Action Plan." International Year of Women's Conference, Houston, Texas, November 18, 1977. (Dorothy I. Height, Covenor, National Council of Negro Women, Washington, D.C., pp. 3-4, 8-12.

22. Ladner, Joyce. *Tomorrow's Tomorrow. The Black Woman.* New York, Doubleday, 1971, p. 277.

23. "Black Women's Action Plan." IYWC. op. cit.

24. "ERA: A Defeat for Women of Color." A Brown Paper by Veronica Collazo and Sharon Parker, published by the National Institute of Women of Color, Washington, D.C., 1984.

25. Ibid.

26. Ibid.

27. "The Trilogy." *For DARK Women and Others: Poems by Satiafa.* Detroit, Michigan, Lotus Press, PO Box 21607, Detroit, Michigan, 48221.

SELECTED REFERENCES

Beale, Frances. "Double Jeopardy: To Be Black and Female," in *The Black Woman*, Toni Cade, Editor. New York, New American Library, 1970.

Billington, Ray Allen, Editor. *The Journal of Charlotte L. Forten. A Free Negro in the Slave Era.* New York, North & Co., 1953.

Blackwell, James E. *The Black Community: Diversity and Unity.* New York, Dodd, Mead & Co., 1975.

Blalock, Hubert M. *Race and Ethnic Relations.* Englewood Cliffs, New Jersey, Prentice-Hall, Inc., 1982.

Blandford, Virginia A., Editor. *Black Women and Liberation Movements.* Washington, D.C., The Institute for the Arts and Humanities, PO Box 723, Howard University.

Blassingame, John W. *The Slave Community. Plantation Life in the Antebellum South.* New York, Oxford University Press, 1979 (Revised and Enlarged Edition).

Brent, Linda. *Incidents in the Life of a Slave Girl .* New York, Harcourt Brace Jovanovich, 1973.

Brownmiller, Susan. *Against Our Will: Men, Women and Rape.* New York, Bantham Books, 1976.

Cade, Toni. *The Black Woman.* New York, New American Library, 1970.

Caplow, Theodore. *Two Against One. Coalitions in Triads.* Englewood Cliffs, New Jersey, Prentice-Hall, 1968.

Collazo, Veronica and Sharon Parker. "ERA: A Defeat For Women of Color." Brown Paper #1 published by the National Institute for Women of Color. Washington, D.C.

Davis, Angela. "Reflections on the Black Woman's Role in the Community of Slaves," in The Black Scholar. December 1971, V3:2-15.

Davis, Angela. *Women, Race and Class* . New York, Random House, 1981.

"Economic Facts on Women of Color." A paper prepared by Phyillis Palmer, George Washington University Women's Studies Program for the National Institute for Women of Color.

French, Laurence. "The Incarcerated Black Female: The Case of Social Double Jeopardy," in *The Black Woman Cross-Culturally*, edited by Filomina C. Steady. Cambridge, Mass., Schenkman Co., 1981.

Giddings, Paula. *When and Where I Enter ... The Impact of Black Women on Race and Sex in America.* New York, William Morrow & Co., 1984.

Gordon, Vivian V. "African American Women: Perceptions of Self and Role." Paper presented to the Association for the Study of Afro-American Life and History, Detroit, 1983. (Available for purchase on cassette.)

Hacker, Helen M. "Sex Roles in Black Society: Caste Versus Caste." Paper presented at the annual meeting of the American Sociological Association. New York, 1973.

Hacker, Helen M. "Class and Race Differences in Gender Roles," in *Gender and Sex in Society*, Lucille Duberman, Editor. New York, Praeger, 1975.

Harley, Sharon and Terborg-Penn, Rosalyn. *The Afro-American Woman. Struggles and Images.* Port Washington, New York, 1978.

Harris, LaDonna. "Introduction." "The Equal Rights Amendment." Statement by Collazo and Parker. Published by the National Institute for Women of Color, Washington, D.C.

Hill, Robert B., Director of Research. *Economic Policies and Black Progress: Myths and Realities* . National Urban League, Washington, D.C. 1981.

Hoctink, H. *Slavery and Race Relations in the Americas* . New York, Harper & Row, 1973.

Hooks, Bell. *Ain't I A Woman. Black Women and Feminism* . Boston, Mass., South End Press, 1981.

Hull, Gloria T.; Bell Scott, Patricia; and Smith, Barbara, Eds. *All the Women Are White, All the Blacks Are Men, But Some of Us Are Brave: Black Women's Studies.* New York, The Feminist Press, 1982.

Jackson, Jacquelyne. "Black Women in a Racist Society," in *Racism and Mental Health,* Charles Willie, et al., Editors. Pittsburgh, University of Pittsburgh Press, 1972.

Joseph, Gloria I., and Lewis, Jill. *Common Differences: Conflicts in Black and White Feminist Perspective*s. Garden City, New York, 1981.

King, Mae C. "The Politics of Sexual Stereotypes," in The Black Scholar. March-April 1973, pp. 12-23.

Ladner, Joyce. *Tomorrow's Tomorrow. The Black Woman.* Garden City, New York, Doubleday & Co., 1971.

Lerner, Gerda. *Black Women in White America.* New York, Vintage Books, 1973.

Loewenberg, Bert James and Bogin, Ruth. *Black Women in 19th Century American Life.* University Park, The Pennsylvania State University Press, 1976.

Noble, Jeanne. *Beautiful, Also, Are the Souls of My Black Sisters.* Englewood Cliffs, New Jersey, 1978.

Reid, Inez Smith. *Together Black Women.* New York, The Third Press, 1972.

Rodgers, Rose, LaFrances, Ed. *The Black Woman.* Beverly Hills, California, Sage Press, 1980.

Staples, Robert. *The Black Woman in America.* Chicago, Nelson Hall, 1979.

Steady, Filomina Chioma, Editor. *The Black Woman Cross-Culturally.* Cambridge, Mass., Schenkman Publishing Co., 1981.

ABOUT THE AUTHOR

Vivian Verdell Gordon is a graduate of Virginia State University (B.S.), the University of Pennsylvania (M.A.) and the University of Virginia (Ph.D.). She was a member of the faculty, Department of Sociology, at the University of Virginia from 1974-1984. During that time, she served for five years (1974-1979) as Chairperson of the Program for Afro-American and African Studies. Recently, Dr. Gordon served as Chairperson and Associate Professor, The Department of African and Afro-American Studies at the State University of New York at Albany. Currently, Dr. Gordon is a visiting professor at Wellesley College, Wellesley, Massachusetts in the Department of Black Studies.

Dr. Gordon's professional background reflects a range of experiences, including work with high school youth through the Upward Bound Program of UCLA, for which she was the initial organizer and the University-community programs coordinated through EPCI (Education Participation in Communities) which she directed at California State University, L.A. Prior to her residence in the Los Angeles community, Dr. Gordon and her family lived in Washington, D.C. where she was a member of the staff of the Congressional Reference Service, during which time she enjoyed a special assignment with the House Committee on Education and Labor, Adam C. Powell, Chairman.

As a more mature woman returning to study for the Ph.D at Virginia, Dr. Gordon focused her graduate research upon those matters which had demanded her attention during her prior extensive work experiences. Her dissertation, later published as *The Self Concept of Black Americans*, resulted from her inquiry into the self perceptions of the Black youth based upon criteria which negated the importance of culture for such young people. She determined that she would contribute to that body of research which would examine new models and paradigms for the assessment and explanation of the African American experience.

This concern about an Afrocentric perspective for the evaluation of Black Americans continues and may be observed in her publications, including her book: *Lectures, Black Scholars on Black Issues* and various articles.

A popular speaker, Dr. Gordon has lectured on many college and university campuses, and she has served variously on such campuses as guest scholar or visiting mentor.

Dr. Gordeon's forthcoming book is: *Black Women in a Typical Town: Perceptions of Role and Self.* It will report her study of African American Women in Muncie, Indiana where she was a part of a research project which concluded in 1983. Specializing in social psychology, Dr. Gordon is among those sociologists who are maintaining an Afrocentric theoretical perspective in the study and presentation of the African American community. She is especially known for her research and her course about Black women.

Under the name, SATIAFA, Ms. Gordon has a poetry collection, *For DARK Women and Others,* available from Lotus Press, Detroit, Michigan. Several of her poems have appeared in Black journals and a second collection AIM FOR THE HEART is to be available soon.